50 pounds less

1.   –Why is your wrist so hurt? +Each time I wanted to quit, I slightly hit myself with a pencil… problem is that it happened three years before I even started to exercise.

2. Neil used to run 8 miles before lunch. According to him, he needed a reason to not feel so guilty for eating one candy a day.

3. Everyone was shocked when Lindsay showed old photos of her when she was fat at the beginning of high school... during her graduation speech.

4. She knew everyone in her family weighed more than 250 pounds. But when she realized she was only 248, it was enough motivation to start with the gym.

5. "Each time I do barrel rolls in my gymnastic class, I pretend to be teleported to another world. This keeps me focus and prepares me to do even more rolls than I actually can."

6. Every kid at school had a dream of become firemen, gardener, chef and teacher. For little Michael, his dream was to avoid his family's heart attack record.

7. –I don't understand, I'm a genie, why don't you just wish to be thin and beautiful? +I think world peace is better; besides, I can get those by myself easily.

8. My dad gave me dumbbells as a child, and thanks to him, I am the most coveted guy in school.

9. My girlfriend told me that she stopped dating her ex because, despite having a good look, he was dumb as a rock. This is the importance of both intelligence and strength.

10. Something changed in Harold's mind when he saw his parent barely moving the table due to the excessive weight. He decided to be stronger to be useful, even if he was just four years old.

11.Jessica thought she couldn't start an exercise routine for being too old. Until she knew her grandma was starting a new one the following week.

12.–How's that Charlie is the best player in the soccer team? I mean, he's like a whale. +He has this thing, how is it called? Oh, talent and discipline.

13. "Hey, remember when you said I was 'too big' for being your girlfriend? Well, now my bed has an Academy Award to fill your place, and he's bigger than you."

14. "Herbs, they said I should try herbs. And after the effects, my house looks like garden."

15. After the kids graduated, Norah didn't have the necessity of walking the mountain to pick them up. Still, she did this for the adrenaline and the nice look in her legs.

16. Each time she had to focus studying, she did 20 push-ups. Now she was both intelligent and ripped.

17. She tricked her children, making them believe that they could drink a 'power energy drink' to be superheroes and exercise better. Years later, they found out that the energy drink was... water.

18.–Hey, you remind me to an ugly kid in my childhood class; and you share the same name, that's crazy because you're hot.

19. My sensei had this motto: "You should be each day faster; so you can run away from pain."

20. The best exercise coach? My dog.

21. Saw this anime series 'One Piece,' and it was so good that I binge watched it entirely. I get rid of like ten pounds. Now it's the training I recommend (and the one I enjoyed the most).

22. My biggest
motivation to keep
working out? The look
in my siblings' eyes
when they see their
buffed brother.

23.—Dude, give me your sister's number, she looks so hot while training in the park.
+Uh… that's my mom, actually.

24. I had to get buffed for this cosplay. Best part was the buffed body couldn't be taken away after the convention ended.

25. After my wife died, I had two choices: To remain alone or to do something, and well… I should go; I have a Ted Talk to do about succeeding in life.

26.–Tell me, what kind of magic trick do you use to lift the car up? +The one consisting on grabbing it with my hands. There's no magic trick, only strength and concentration.

27. "I know! I will do a YouTube channel consisting in both exercise and makeup. It will be for both men and women... Oh, geez, I already have 400K subs!"

28. Johnny buffed up for his girlfriend, but they broke up. Now he's dating his ex's sister, and she is jealous as hell.

29. "Wow, I didn't believe you were like that under the three-size-bigger shirt."

30. "And remember, kiddo, life was made to live it by your own rules" (he said after his fifth heart attack that year... and it was only April.)

31. He thought by watching horror movies he would burn more calories than with a single gym routine. Now he was fat *and* scared.

32. "I don't know, man, this 'getting you face full of bees to get thinner' doesn't look quite scientific. This has to do with that fact that I'm dating your ex?"

33.—I can't believe you eat all those vegetables. What are you? Vegan, hahaha. +No, dude, I just like green foods.

34. "It's amazing, I was two years on the gym and nothing happened, but I went to the bath and I got rid of three pounds?"

35. Little did we know, by Jamie liking the Power Rangers as a child and imitating their stunts he would be quite a great gymnast.

36. Harold had to break up because of his health. But he always considered his job as his true (toxic) lover.

37. "It's not fair, I've read many books about weight loss, but none of them told me I had to do something about working out."

38. "Son, our family has this terrible condition that in most of the cases can be lethal. Bright side is that it starts at age 90, and we always manage to get there."

39. I tried flamenco dancing, and I now understand why that people is always thin.

40. I made a diet consisting on adding a condiment to every food. Apparently, this thing is so disgusting that you are forced to not eating it at all.

41.–But mom, I actually managed to get thinner. +But you're using drugs, Adrian, that's not the honest way.

42. "You know what's sad? Everyone flirting with me for my body, but what about my feelings? I try to work them out too."

43. "Looks like you're not fat... congratulations, it's a girl."

44. It's amazing what you can do eating a fruit a day. I even won lottery… that doesn't have to do with anything, but it tastes good.

45.–I gained more weight? But I always do exercise! +Playing FIFA it's not considered as physical sport.

46. I tricked my best friend to start gym instead of me for a stupid promotion. Now I'm the one who gets the ugly friend. Thanks, me.

47. "What's this about been buffed up for the cameras? I mean, I thought this was a record label."

48.–The secret for these muscles is drinking water from the Himalayas during summer. +Wow, really? –No, dummy, it's to simply work out…

49.—Why is everyone looking at me so weirdly? Haven't you seen someone in her sport outfit? +Sure, Miss Brown, but do you think you should come to school like that?

50. "Apparently, I have to eat more junk food to avoid my bulimia... I just ate my first hamburger, and I say: Bring it on!"